A Guide to the
FREE CHURCH OF SCOTLAND
College and Offices

William S Anderson

KNOX PRESS [EDINBURGH]

Dedicated to the memory of John Maitland (1803-1865)
Accountant-General to the Court of Session

KNOX PRESS (EDINBURGH)
15 North Bank Street, Edinburgh EH1 2LS

© Free Church of Scotland 1994
First published in 1994

ISBN 0 904422 56 9

Photography by George T Thomson LRPS and Walter Bell LRPS

Design by Mark Blackadder

Printed and bound in Great Britain by McCorquodale (Scotland) Ltd

Introduction

The building on the Mound which houses the Theological College, General Offices and Bookshop of the Free Church of Scotland is a prominent material monument to the legal recognition of the post-1900 Church's claim to preserve the constitution and identity of the 1843 Church of Scotland Free. No mere monument to the past, it is central to much of the ongoing activity of the denomination. In addition to those who study and work here, or who come on Church business, the building is visited by many who are interested in its library, architecture, decoration, Disruption painting, significant portraits or varied history.

This guide will be of interest and use to many throughout the Church who have never been able to visit 15 North Bank Street though the address has been well known to them since youth. It will also inform those who tour the building and will provide an attractive memento of their visit.

Mr W S Anderson, College Curator and Offices Caretaker since 1974, except for eighteen months, is an authority on the building and its contents, and on the social, civil and ecclesiastical history of Edinburgh. He has answered the questions of many who have enjoyed his guided tours. This guide records some of the information passed on by him. Its publication is also a tribute from the Church to one whose diligent and devoted service has contributed significantly to the smooth conduct of the business transacted within these walls and to the good public relations of the Church.

HUGH M CARTWRIGHT
Free Church College
1 July 1994

ABOVE
Royal Coat of Arms of
King James VI and I,
as portrayed in the
Architect's Window.

The Beginnings

In 1722, Sir John Lauder of Woodhead, Lord Fountainhall, died at the age of seventy-six. It was customary, on being appointed a Senator of the College of Justice, for a person to take the name of the estate or lands associated with him. To say the least it would have been ridiculous for Sir John Lauder to take the title 'Lord Woodhead', so Fountainhall was selected instead.

For most of his legal life, Lord Fountainhall lived in a house on the site of the present building, and here he died. This house, built in the middle of the sixteenth century, survived until 1725, when all but part of the northern wall was demolished to make way for James Brownhill's tenement or land. The house can be seen in its entirety in the drawing by John Slezer.

Lord Fountainhall had a distinguished legal career. He was made a Lord of Justiciary in 1690, and shortly afterwards declined the position of Lord Advocate. Fountainhall defended Archibald Campbell, 9th Earl of Argyll, with such success that the Earl escaped for a short time. He was engaged in the interests of the Duchess in the defence of the Duke of Monmouth, for which he incurred the displeasure of the court of James VII and II. Lord Fountainhall voted against the Union of 1707.

In 1839, the last of his Lordship's great great grandchildren, Miss Innes of Stowe, died. She remembered her grandmother telling her of visits she paid to her venerable grandfather in the old house. The main room of the house was covered in gilt leather, and the room was full of dark oak presses, one of which was ornamented with a death's head mask. On leaving, her grandfather presented the little girl with a shilling which the serving maid immediately appropriated for her own use.

In 1982, when renovation work was taking place within the Free Church Bookshop, a wall of the sixteenth century dwelling was revealed, showing a fine pointed window of the period.

OPPOSITE, TOP
Drawing of Edinburgh (c1705) by John Slezer, showing Lord Fountainhall's house.

OPPOSITE, BOTTOM
View from James Court, looking North, 1775.

James Brownhill's Building

Within three years of Lord Fountainhall's death, the old house and those immediately beside it were purchased by James Brownhill, a local speculator/ builder, and were almost wholly demolished. By 1727, Brownhill was to erect what were to become the luxury flats of the day, and the last great tenement built in the old town of Edinburgh prior to the rise of the New Town, or Classical Edinburgh, in 1767. He named the building James Court, after himself.

The tenement was to be eight levels and a garret in height. Each flat, or apartment, consisted of five rooms and a kitchen, there being no running water or sanitary facilities. The principal bedroom was the receiving room. In certain north facing rooms, there were small narrow closets for private prayer: *'when thou prayest, enter into thy closet'* (Matthew 6:6). The closets on the south front were kept for the powdering of the periwig. Between the hours of 10pm and 7am, it was possible for the garbage and refuse, collected within the building, to be piled in the courtyard for uplifting. A man was employed to carry water and to look after the building as a whole.

Among the more famous people to occupy the building was David Hume, the philosopher, who purchased a double flat in 1762. This was situated in the western portion of the building on the third floor from the courtyard, and was entered by the west stair. Hume was in residence in James Court for only a short time when he was appointed Secretary to the British Embassy in Paris. In his absence, Hume let his flat to his friend, Dr Blair. It is interesting to find Hume writing from Paris to his friend, Dr Ferguson, *'I am sensible that I am misplaced, and I wish twice or thrice a day for my easy chair and my retreat in James Court.'* Then he adds the beautiful sentence, *'Never think , dear Ferguson , that as long as you are master of your own fireside and your own time , you can be unhappy, or that any other circumstances can add to your enjoyment.'*

In one of his letters to Dr Blair at James Court, Hume writes, *'Never put a fire in*

OPPOSITE
*James Court in 1844, in
proximity to the site of
New College.*

the south room with the red paper. It is so warm of itself that all last winter, which was a very severe one, I lay with a single blanket, and frequently, upon coming in at midnight starving with cold, have sat down and read for an hour, as if I had had a stove in the room.'

We find Hume again at James Court in 1769, having returned from Paris, writing to Adam Smith who was then beginning his great work, *The Wealth of Nations*, in the quiet of his mother's home in Kirkcaldy, *'I am glad to have come to within sight of you, and to have a view of Kirkcaldy from my windows, but I wish also to be within speaking terms of you.'*

Within a year, Hume moved to the New Town, to a more elegant flat in North St David Street, so named, by a wag, after Hume himself.

In 1770, we find James Boswell of Auchinleck living in David Hume's house, and here, in August of that year, he entertained that great man of letters, Dr Samuel Johnson, prior to their visit to the Hebrides. Boswell did not reside long in James Court, as we find him in London shortly afterwards.

With the development of the New Town, the building began to decline, and by the turn of the 18th century it had deteriorated.

On 15 August 1857, the western half of the building was gutted by fire and almost a hundred people were made homeless. There was no loss of life, and it is recorded that there were many heroic acts of rescue.

From shortly after 1843, the Free Church of Scotland offices were at 58 Frederick Street, now occupied by Balfour and Manson, Solicitors. This building, although attractive, was becoming quite inadequate for the large and growing denomination.

Early in 1858, a prominent Free Churchman, Mr John Maitland, Accountant General to the Court of Session, realising the importance of the site, and being a step ahead of his colleagues, purchased James Court and decided to rebuild the western portion of the building. The site was ideal in every way. It was prominently situated on the edge of the Old Town, overlooking the New Town, and the main advantage was that it adjoined the New College Divinity Hall and the Assembly Hall.

The architect chosen by Mr Maitland was David Cousin. He was born in Leith, the son of a joiner, and was later apprenticed to the eminent Scottish architect, William Playfair who had designed New College, in the Tudor style, for the Free Church. David Cousin's most important projects for the Free Church up to that time were Kingston

ABOVE

A door pediment in the Presbytery Hall in the style of Grinling Gibbons, late 17th early 18th century.

OPPOSITE, TOP

Drawing by Skene showing the building as it was c1800.

OPPOSITE, BOTTOM

Etching by D O Hill showing the building on fire. 15 August 1857.

Church, Glasgow, and Free St George's, Edinburgh, for Dr Candlish. This church stood where the Caledonian Hotel is today, but it was demolished twenty years after it was built. The tower of the building is incorporated within a sheltered housing complex in Raeburn Place, Edinburgh. The style accepted by John Maitland for the new Free Church Offices was Scottish Baronial, and by the spring of 1862 the building was ready for occupation. The total cost was £6,000, the whole of which was borne by the donor.

In 1887, the top two floors of the eastern part of the building, which had been used by the Guild of Bakers as a Guildhall, were taken into use by the church as extra committee and despatch rooms. Prior to this, in 1874, Dr Black, the librarian of New College (a blind man!), who had lived for twelve years in what is now the caretaker's flat, moved out because of the risk of fire. The staircase at the west end of the building was removed, and internal strong rooms were inserted. They were removed in 1975 to make way for the present fire escape.

RIGHT
Presbytery Hall ceiling roundels.

Distinctive Rooms

Perhaps John Maitland's most impressive gift to the church was the magnificent PRESBYTERY HALL, built in the Victorian revival 17th century Jacobean style, measuring 58 feet in length, 28 feet in width, and with a ceiling height of 23 feet. One has a feeling of overwhelming grandeur on seeing the room for the first time. The panelling is of Oregon pine, which must have been from one of the first shiploads of the wood to enter Britain from North America. The panels are of various

LEFT
Presbytery Hall.

widths, several being 5 feet 6 inches, denoting the great width of the parent tree. Above the doorways, of which there are four in the room, are fine carvings in the style of Grinling Gibbons, the 17th century English wood carver, depicting wreaths of flowers and fruits mingling with laurel leaves. These carvings are much earlier than the building, and may be of late 17th or early 18th century origin.

The chief glory of the room is, undoubtedly, the ceiling, modelled by hand: a wonderful example of the Victorian plasterer's craft. There is a heavy cornice with heraldic devices picked out in various colours – predominantly soft green, brown, red and white. The original colours of the ceiling were white and gold. The gold leaf which remains today is that of 1862, and is as fresh as it was on the day it was applied.

The original Axminster carpet, measuring 35 feet by 17 feet, cost £45, the account for which is still in existence. This carpet was replaced in 1993. It is interesting to note that the large committee table – a fine piece of Victorian craftsmanship – has not been removed from the hall since the day it was first placed in position.

In 1900, the majority of the Free Church of Scotland joined with the United Presbyterian Church to form the United Free Church of Scotland. The minority who dissented from the union continued as the Free Church of Scotland. Because the United Free Church was a much larger body, it was necessary to enlarge the office space; so in 1902, the remaining part of the early Georgian building was brought into use, and fairly extensive alterations were carried out. The corridor walls on the south side of the building were altered, and much plain Art Nouveau glass was installed. It is reasonable to say that this building has more of this type of glass than has any other building in Edinburgh. It was at this time that five important fireplaces, in the style of Robert Adam, were installed. An elevator was added and is still in use. The fine entrance doorway was moved twelve feet east to provide entry from the earlier building.

The Free Church minority appealed to have their position as the rightful successors to the Free Church of 1843 established and won their case in 1904 after appeal to the House of Lords. In 1905 the Churches (Scotland) Act set up a Royal Commission, under the chairmanship of the 9th Earl of Elgin, to divide the properties between the two denominations. In 1906 the Elgin Commission awarded to the Free Church of Scotland the building at 15 North Bank Street (formerly James Court) as their College

RIGHT

Chalmers Hall.
Chalmers Hall looking West,
formerly the Ladies Missionary
Society Hall. Since 1907, the
College Common Hall. The Free
Church heritage collection of books
and manuscripts is contained in
the cases which line the South
walls. The large canvas above the
fireplace is late 16th century in
origin, and portrays several of the
Reformers including Melanchthon
and Zwingli. This picture was
given to the Church by Sheriff
Maitland Heriot.

LEFT
Senate Hall.
The business of the College is
conducted in this fine early 18th
century room. The cases contain
the more valuable books in the
library collection – fine 17th
century early Puritan works; early
18th century rarities; and the
small, but important, collection of
Gaelic literature. The portraits
above the fireplaces are those of Dr
James Duff MacCulloch, Principal
of the Free Church College,
1905-1926, by Henry Wright
Kerr RSA (1857-1936); and Dr
William Cunningham, Principal
of New College, 1847-1861,
by Norman MacBeth RSA
(1821-1888).

The room contains a fine
Victorian committee table; en suite
are twelve splendid, walnut-framed
chairs, carved in Gothic design
(c1860).

RIGHT

College Dining Room.
From early in the 19th century to
1887 this was the hall of the
Guild of Bakers. The room is
panelled in light oak; the ceiling is
a masterpiece of the plasterer's art,
and is of a complicated
mathematical design. The portraits
above the fireplaces are of Dr John
Bruce, by Norman MacBeth RSA
(1821–1888), perhaps the finest
portrait in the building; and Dr
Samuel Miller, also by Norman
MacBeth. Dr Bruce was minister
of St Andrew's Church of
Scotland, George Street,
Edinburgh at the time of the
Disruption in 1843, and Dr
Miller was minister of St
Matthew's Free Church,
Glasgow.

and Offices. On 8 January 1907 the Free Church repossessed the building which they formerly owned.

For the best part of seventy years little was done to the structure of the building. In the summer of 1975 an extensive scheme of restoration and renovation was commenced. Among other improvements the electrical system was completely re-wired, and the ornamental pediments on the north side, which had greatly deteriorated, were replaced, but in a different design showing a rose and thistle motif. Later, a fire alarm system was installed.

On 20 October 1978 a service of thanksgiving was held in the Presbytery Hall. There was a large and representative congregation present including the Moderator of the Assembly, Rev H M Ferrier; the Earl of Crawford and Balcarres, Chairman of the Historic and Ancient Monuments Commission (Scotland); and Bailie John Gray, on behalf of Edinburgh City Council. Principal James Mackintosh preached the sermon, his text being Psalm 127:1, *'Except the Lord build the house, they labour in vain that build it.'*

N I S I   D O M I N U S   F R U S T R A

BELOW
Presbyterian Ridge, showing the building as it is today.

The First General Assembly
of the Free Church of Scotland

Signing the Act of Separation and Deed of Demission, 23 May 1843

D O Hill R S A (1802 – 1870)

In the Assembly Reports of 1866, we find Dr Candlish recommending to the General Assembly of that year that they purchase Mr D O Hill's memorable and unique painting of the first General Assembly of the Free Church of Scotland. In Dr Candlish's words he had no doubt that *'some of their American friends would like to acquire it and convey it across the Atlantic,'* therefore he would not wonder *'though they had competitors for the picture.'* In any event a public appeal was made to the church at large, and this great work, which occupied the artist for twenty-three years, was bought for the church at a cost of £1,500.

A few days after the Assembly met at Tanfield in 1843, D O Hill approached Dr Robert Gordon of the High Church, Edinburgh, and showed him a small sketch which he had prepared of a proposed painting of the great event. Dr Gordon appreciated the importance of the proposed picture, but suggested that it should represent *'something that would signify the completion of the Disruption, such as the signing of the Deed of Demission.'* This suggestion carried such a conviction in the mind of the artist that he at once adopted it and remodelled the plan of the picture. The preliminary sketch made by Hill and shown to Dr Gordon was purchased by the Trustees in 1903 and placed in the Presbytery Hall.

David Octavius Hill was eminently qualified to paint such a picture. He was a trained artist and a profound and serious-minded Free Churchman, having lived through the Ten Years' Conflict and been an eye-witness to the event. He portrays himself in the picture, sketch book in hand.

Much has been written about the picture over the years, and it is now of international repute, due to the fact that it is regarded as the first canvas ever painted with the use of a camera. Principal Brewster of the University of Edinburgh,

OPPOSITE

Protest, read by Dr David Welsh, retiring Moderator, in St Andrew's Church, George Street, 18 May 1843.

We the undersigned Ministers and Elders chosen as Commissioners to the General Assembly of the Church of Scotland indicted to meet this day but precluded from holding the said Assembly by reason of the circumstances herein after set forth, in consequence of which a Free Assembly of the Church of Scotland in accordance with the laws and constitution of the said Church cannot at this time be holden, Considering that the Legislature, by their rejection of the Claim of Right adopted by the last General Assembly of the said Church, and their refusal to give redress and protection against the jurisdiction assumed, and the coercion of late repeatedly attempted to be exercised over the courts of the Church in matters spiritual by the Civil Court, have recognized and fixed the conditions of the Church Establishment, as henceforward to subsist in Scotland, to be such as those have been pronounced and declared by the said Civil Court in their several recent decisions in regard to matters spiritual and ecclesiastical; Whereby it has been held inter alia.

1. That the courts of the Church by Law established and members thereof are liable to be coerced by the Civil Courts in the exercise of their spiritual functions ...

2. That the said Civil Court have power to interfere with and control the preaching of the Gospel and administration of ordinances as authorised and enjoined by the Church Courts of the Establishment.

3. That the said Civil Court have power to suspend spiritual censures pronounced by the Church Courts of the Establishment against the Ministers and Probationers of the Church ...

4. That the said Civil Court have power to reduce and set aside the sentences of the Church Courts of the Establishment deposing Ministers from the office of the Holy Ministry, and depriving Probationers of their licence to preach the Gospel ...

5. That the said Civil Court have power to determine on the right to sit as Members of the Judicatories of this Church by Law established and to issue interdicts against sitting and voting therein ...

... from the now enforced separation from an Establishment which we have prized, though, through inference with conscience, the sickness done to us proceeds from ...

David Welsh, Modr.

Thomas Chalmers Minr	C. Maxwell Elder
Henry Grey Minr	Robt Brydon Minr
Patrick ...	John R MacKenzie Minr
Walter Tait Minr	Robt Crawford Minr
Robert ... Minister	James MacKenzie Minister
...	Philip Forsyth Elder
Robert Candlish Minr	Robert ... Elder
James ...	Wm ... Elder
Robert Elder ...	Thomas B. Bell Minr
... Elder	Mathew Kirkland Minister
...	Claud Alexander Elder
John Thomson Minr	David Landsborough Minister
W. Bruce Cunningham Minr	Matthew Dickie Minister
John ...	...
Andrew Baird Minr	...
John Wallace Minr	W. ... Crawford Elder
John ...	P. B. Muir Minister Elder
George Fuller ...	Robert Smith Minr
Geo. Harkness Minister	Duncan McFarlan Minr
Henry Duncan Minister	J. Macaulay ... Minister

ABOVE

*A preliminary sketch
by D O Hill.*

LEFT

*First General Assembly of
The Free Church of Scotland
signing the Act of Separation
and Deed of Demission,
23 May 1843.
Painted by D O Hill RSA
(1802 – 1870).*

realising the tremendous difficulty there would be in painting such a large group of people, introduced D O Hill to Fox Talbot's calotype process, which was the first type of photograph which could be repeated from a negative. In actual fact, Hill did much of the pioneer work in this method of photography. The somewhat earlier Daguerreotype was a more laborious process and not suitable for the task. Hill and his young friend, Dr Robert Adamson, immediately set to work photographing the subjects: Dr Gordon was certainly the first.

The picture, albeit, is not factual but commemorative, and shows 457 out of the 1,500 people who attended the opening of the Assembly. The main character is, of course, Dr Thomas Chalmers, who has the central position. Space does not allow us to describe the painting in full, nor to give a biographical sketch of even a few of the characters represented. Such personalities as Dr David Welsh, Dr Patrick MacFarlan and Principal William Cunningham are well known. Let us, however, mention some of the lesser known people represented: Dr Lyman Beecher, the father of Harriet Beecher Stowe who wrote *Uncle Tom's Cabin*; Dr Merle D'Aubigne of Geneva, who wrote the *History of the Reformation*; Dr Adolphe Sydow, Chaplain to the King of Prussia, who reported on the Assembly to Queen Victoria and Prince Albert; Sir Thomas MacDougall Brisbane, Bart., President of the Royal Society, who gave his name to the city of Brisbane in Australia; Dr James McCosh, who became President of Princeton University, USA, a post held at one time by Jonathan Edwards; Sir John Harvey, President of the Royal Scottish Academy; the Hon Miss MacKenzie of Seaforth with her ear trumpet; and Lady Emma Campbell of Argyll.

It must be remembered that D O Hill did not paint every character from calotypes. Many were painted from life as they appeared in 1843, and others as they appeared later in life, with grey hair and white beards. There are a number of anachronisms in the picture: for instance, Dr Duff of the India Mission was in India at the time of the Disruption and Dr John (Rabbi) Duncan was in Budapest. Mr Hately, the Assembly Precentor, was at business that day, a day which was dull and showery, but as the fathers and brethren joined in singing the opening verses of Psalm 43, '*O send Thy light forth and Thy truth…*', the sunlight burst through and flooded the gathering. This was taken as a blessing from God on the proceedings.

The National Covenant of 1638

If one includes the large and varied collection of pamphlets dating from the late 16th century; the fine library of Celtic literature, which contains the exceedingly rare Gaelic Catechism of 1660 of which there are only three copies in existence; and the many 16th and 17th century commentaries in their original calf bindings, the entire catalogue amounts to some 20,000 items. Although it is small compared to some other important libraries, it is in itself a notable and fine collection.

Perhaps the most poignant of the historic items on display is the National Covenant of 1638. This document, measuring 37 by 27 inches, was bequeathed to the church by the 11th Earl of Dalhousie on his death in 1874. It was placed in the Presbytery Hall in 1906 and has remained there ever since. Although in itself not unique, there being several extant manuscripts in public and private collections, this parchment is particularly interesting because of its fine condition and the clarity of its text. It would appear to have been signed at a field conventicle in Ayrshire.

The first of the National Covenants was signed in late February 1638, within Greyfriars Church, Edinburgh. It was composed by Johnston of Warriston and Henderson of Leuchars, as legal advisers, and revised by Lords Rothes, Balmerino and Loudon. It was said that 60,000 people thronged the streets of Edinburgh that day. After the initial signing, copies were sent all over the country and were subscribed by aristocrats, ministers, and thousands of ordinary people. This National Covenant and the movement behind it won for us, at the cost of some 18,000 lives, religious freedom, and made the nation in the centuries that followed truly great and God-fearing.

In his book *The Winning of the West*, President Theodore Roosevelt expresses thus the debt his countrymen owe to the 17th and 18th century Scots: *'It is doubtful if we have realised in the leadership of our country, the part played by that stern and virile people, the*

ABOVE

Some of the many signatories of the National Covenant of 1638.

RIGHT

The National Covenant of 1638. According to modern historical research, the text of the Covenant formed the basis of the American Bill of Rights, 1776.

Scots-Irish, whose predecessors taught the creed of Knox and Calvin. They became the vanguard of our civilization ... these were the men who first declared for American independence ... they were the kinsfolk of the Covenanters, they deemed it a religious duty to interpret their own Bible ... for generations their whole ecclesiastical and scholastic systems have been found fundamentally democratic.'

On our Covenant, among the signatures of the Scottish peerage, we see that of the first Earl of Dalhousie whose descendant, the Hon Fox Maule (Fox, after the great Whig politician, Charles James Fox), was to leave this parchment to the Free Church of Scotland. There are few names more identified with the history of the Free Church than that of this distinguished 19th century nobleman. It is impossible here to enumerate in full his many and great services to the Free Church. Fox Maule was chosen as the man to whom the Church could safely entrust the advocacy of her righteous cause to Parliament. He discharged himself of this obligation admirably. Having accepted the principles of the Free Church as true and right, he threw himself heartily into the struggle and sacrifices of the Disruption period, and continued to be the steadfast and generous friend of the cause to the end of his life. It is recorded that Dalhousie, on his death-bed, called for his minister and for a young footman who had come to a saving knowledge of the truth and in whom he had shown a tender interest. Giving them his hands, the nobleman, young servant and pastor drew near to the Mercy Seat in prayer, to find help in time of need. This great man had a most solemn passing. His minister read to him from John 11:25-26, *'Jesus said unto her, "I am the resurrection and the life ..."'*, and when he came to the end of the second verse: *'"Believest thou this?"'*, Dalhousie stretched forth both of his arms as if to welcome his Lord, and then, almost immediately, departed to be with Him.

The Architect's Window and the Memorial or Moncrieff Window

O f the 163 windows of varying size which allow daylight to penetrate the fastness of this fortress-like building, two attract much attention. The former, measuring 7'6" by 6", with three lights or panels, was a gift from the architect of the Victorian part of this building, Mr David Cousin. The aperture in which the window is placed was originally meant as a doorway to the passage leading to the Presbytery Hall from James Court. It was thought, however, on completion of the building, that the Free Church Officer would have too many doors to attend to, hence the stained glass window.

It is extremely difficult to describe adequately the colours in a stained glass window. Like all windows of this type, it is better seen on a sunny day. Crimson, blues and browns are the predominant colours. The first panel depicts Sir David Lindsay of the Mount, famous for his satire, *The Three Estaites*. The central panel shows James VI and I with crown, sceptre and orb, wearing the imperial mantle. The third panel depicts George Buchanan, James's tutor as a child, carrying the Bible in his left hand and wearing the gown of a scholar. Buchanan was a correspondent of Erasmus, and was the only layman to become Moderator of the Church of Scotland. He was regarded as the foremost Latin scholar of his day.

Like other ornamental parts of this building, the window is ablaze with heraldic devices: the arms of the King of Scots before 1603, the arms of Great Britain after 1603, and the arms of the Lindsays. The large lintel topping this window on the outside bears the inscription in Latin, *Nisi Dominus Frustra* (except the Lord build the house, they labour in vain that build it). There is an anchor centralised under the text, signifying the anchor of the soul, and the initials FC-PH 1862 are on either side of it, sometimes confused by the Edinburgh City tourist guides as a marriage lintel. Generations of Edinburgh children who lived in James Court have designated the three figures as the

TOP

John Knox, taken from the Memorial or Moncrieff Window.

ABOVE

Sir Henry Moncrieff, taken from the Memorial or Moncrieff Window.

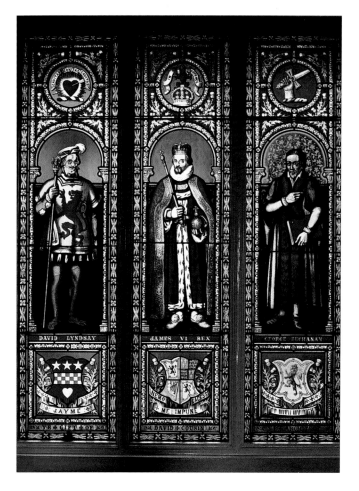

ABOVE

Architect's window.

ABOVE

Memorial or Moncrieff window.

three kings.

The Memorial window is the larger of the two windows and is situated at the West end of the Presbytery Hall, measuring 11'3" by 11'. It was made, like the Architect's window, by Ballantyne and Sons of Leith, and was installed in 1862. This famous firm specialised in stained glass windows, and was responsible for their design and manufacture at home and abroad. The glass in this window is particularly thin, but extremely beautiful in design and colour. There are nine medallion portraits in this window, each being 23" in diameter and, in their size and structure, similar to those in the Magdalen Chapel, Edinburgh, so well known to lovers of the Reformed faith.

This window has been known for many years as the Memorial or Moncrieff window. The central panel bears the portrait of Sir Henry Wellwood Moncrieff DD, who died in 1827, some 35 years before the window was installed. He was Moderator of the General Assembly of the Church of Scotland in 1785. His grandson, Sir Henry Wellwood Moncrieff was Moderator of the Free Church of Scotland General Assembly in 1869, and died in 1883. This window is a memorial to those who held the torch of truth for the 300 years prior to the Disruption of 1843.

The portrait in the first panel is that of George Wishart who was martyred in 1546, followed by John Knox (1505-1572), the great Reformer. The next two panels show portraits of Alexander Henderson (1583-1646), known as the 'Lion of the Covenant', and John Erskine DD (1721-1803), a leading theologian of the day. In the remaining four panels there are portraits of Andrew Thomson DD (1779-1831), minister of St George's, Edinburgh, who wrote the famous Psalm tune of that name, Thomas McCrie DD (1772-1835), Church historian and biographer of John Knox; Thomas Chalmers DD (1780-1847), the first Moderator of the Free Church of Scotland, 1843; and William Cunningham DD (1805-1861), Principal of New College and a leading theologian.

This lovely window enhances the dignity of the Presbytery Hall, and has, like the rest of the building, a marked Scottish flavour with its entwining Scots thistles and Saltire design framing the portraits of these great men. A verse from Scripture reads, *'Fear God, Honour the King'*, and can be seen directly below the portrait of Thomas Chalmers. The cost of the window was £150.

ABOVE

Thomas Chalmers DD,
taken from the Memorial or
Moncrieff Window.

The Disruption Brooch

In its collections, the Free Church has two specimens of this rare piece of the silver-smith's art. One is worn by the wife of the current Moderator of the General Assembly. It is thought that there are only 35 left out of a possible 235.

The brooch first appeared in 1845 and was patented by the firm of Middleton Rettie, Jeweller, Aberdeen, who was probably the mind behind the project. The firm of Alexander Kirkwood cast the die for the brooch, and it was sold by two Edinburgh firms, Naysmith and Co., and Marshall and Sons.

To Victorian ladies, these brooches were practical and attractive ornaments for their shawls. The Hon Miss Mackenzie of Seaforth can be seen wearing the brooch in the Disruption painting. What motive lay behind the wearing of the brooch is found in a poem published in Hugh Miller's *Witness* on 11 February 1846. The first verse is printed alongside.

Wear the jewel, lady!
Wear it on thy breast,
Openly to God and man
Be the truth confest!
Tremble not to stand avowed
For the cause we love;
Openly the faithful ones
Shall be owned above.

LEFT.
The Disruption Brooch
(showing both sides).

TOP, LEFT

Parian bust of Dr Alexander Duff (1806-1878) made by Spode.

TOP, MIDDLE

Marble bust of Principal William Cunningham (1805-1861) by Sir John Steell.

TOP, RIGHT

Marble bust (posthumous) of Dr David Welsh (1793-1845) by William Brodie A.R.S.A.

BOTTOM

The MacNeilage Casket. Solid silver casket, Art Nouveau style, Glasgow, 1918, presented to Mr Archibald MacNeilage from Friends in the Free Church of Scotland.

Biographical Sketches

There have been many outstanding characters who have lived or worked in the building. We have space to select only four: two 19th century characters, and two from the 20th century. The two former personages have their association with the Disruption and beyond.

1. Our first sketch is of *Alexander Stocks*, friend and confidant of Dr John Bruce, minister of St Andrew's Church, George Street, Edinburgh, where the General Assembly met in 1843. He was a comb-maker, and was converted under the ministry of Dr Bruce. He was responsible for the seating arrangements at Tanfield Hall where the first General Assembly of the Free Church met on 18 May 1843. He later became Senior Officer of Assembly and was Church Officer of Free St Andrew's where Dr Bruce was minister. In 1862, Mr Stocks became Free Church Officer, as it was then known, of the new Free Church Offices on the Mound, and died there in 1881.

Alexander Stocks was a man of sterling Christian character and the greatest kindliness. Such was the bond between him and Dr Bruce, that it is recorded on one occasion that the learned minister, whose memory was failing due to advancing years, forgot to take a service for a colleague, and on apologising to him in a letter, wrote: *'I was so ashamed that I did not even tell Stocks'*. On committee days, Stocks would take his position at the top of the stairs leading to the second floor corridor, and there greet the members. He was often asked his views on matters relating to Church policy and he did not hesitate to give them, sometimes at great length. Mr Stocks lived for only three months after the death of Dr Bruce and was interred in the New Calton burying ground, Edinburgh. The present writer has tried, unsuccessfully, to locate his grave, but it would appear that there is no stone over it. We can truly say that Alexander Stocks came to his grave in full age, *'like as a shock of corn cometh in in his season'* (Job 5:26).

2. On entering the vestibule of the Free Church building, one is immediately faced with a striking three-quarter length portrait of a Victorian gentleman. The subject

TOP
Roderick MacLeod of Snizort.
Artist unknown.

BOTTOM
Mrs Ann R MacLeod of Snizort.
Artist unknown.

TOP ROW, LEFT
Dr Patrick MacFarlan by William Bonnar RSA (1800-1853). Dr MacFarlan signed away the richest living in the Church of Scotland in 1843.

TOP ROW, RIGHT
Dr Thomas Chalmers, after Sir John Watson Gordon RA(1788-1864). First Moderator of the Free Church of Scotland, 1843.

MIDDLE ROW, LEFT
Dr John Bruce by Norman MacBeth RSA (1821-1888). Presentation portrait in the 50th year of his ministry.

MIDDLE ROW, CENTRE
Mr John Maitland by Norman MacBeth RSA (1821-1888).

MIDDLE ROW, RIGHT
Mr John MacDonald by James Irvine RSA (1824-1889). Retiral portrait.

BOTTOM ROW, LEFT
Principal John MacLeod by David Foggie RSA (1878-1948). Portrait of the year, Royal Scottish Academy 1945.

BOTTOM ROW, RIGHT
Dr Donald MacLean by David Foggie RSA (1878-1948).

is *John MacDonald*, the first General Treasurer of the Free Church of Scotland, 1843-81.

Mr MacDonald was a strong, fearless man, of great character and charm, with firm commitment to his work, believing that whatever he did was done unto the Lord. He took an active part in many revival movements, and was closely associated with William Chalmers Burns, who decided to go to China while he was a guest in Mr MacDonald's home. Foreign students attending New College were the object of much of his care and some of them were deeply indebted to him for spiritual help.

John MacDonald was keenly interested in sailing, and liked nothing better than to adjourn to the Forth and sail his gallant little craft, the *Strathnaver*. Usually at the helm was the aforementioned Alexander Stocks – his loyal helmsman, both afloat and ashore.

On Mr MacDonald's death, Rev J G Cunningham of St Luke's, who was with him at the end, wrote of that *'serious piety which carried him through fifty years of arduous labour with fidelity, through many months of lingering illness with patience, and into the valley of death without fear'*.

'Be thou faithful unto death, and I will give thee a Crown of life' (Rev 2:10).

3. Since 1906, one of the most revered of the College Principals was *Dr John Macleod*. When he was translated to the Church triumphant on 11 July 1948, the Scottish Church lost one of her most remarkable sons, a man whose encyclopaedic knowledge was drawn upon, and whose ripe judgement was appealed to, not only by his brethren in the Free Church of Scotland, but by representatives of the various branches of the Reformed Churches in many lands.

John Macleod was a native of Fort William, where he had his early education. At the age of thirteen, he enrolled at the Old Grammar School in Aberdeen, and although younger than most of his classmates, he soon became first in attainment, particularly in the Classics, and was Dux of the School. At nineteen he graduated from Aberdeen University with First Class Honours in Classics, having obtained the premier awards in the ancient languages. His professors urged him to proceed to Oxford and Cambridge, but John MacLeod had already laid his resplendent gifts on God's altar and coveted for himself, as the supreme honour of his life, the service of his Divine Master in the ministry of the Word.

In order to widen his usefulness in the pulpit, John Macleod learnt Gaelic, and

ABOVE
Professor's study showing fireplace by Robert Adam (1728-1792) and Victorian mirror in the style of Robert Adam.

TOP

'Leaving the Manse' by
Sir George Harvey PRSA
(1806-1876).

BOTTOM

Minutes of Convocation held in
Roxburgh Church, Edinburgh,
November 1842.

became an authority on the subject. He taught in the Nicolson Institute, Stornoway, for over a year, and then resumed his studies for the ministry, first at New College, Edinburgh, and then at Assembly's College, Belfast.

At the Declaratory Act crisis in 1893, John Macleod sided with the Free Presbyterian party and in 1897 was ordained and inducted to the pastorate of Lochbroom. Four years later he was translated to Kames. While he was there, and following the Church Union of 1900, he gave valuable service as lecturer to the students of the remanent Free Church: and in 1906, after his admission to the Free Church, he was appointed to the Chair of Greek and New Testament Exegesis in the reconstituted Free Church College. In 1913, he was translated to the Free North Church, Inverness. In 1927 he was appointed Principal of the College, remaining at the Free North until 1930, when the College reclaimed him as Professor of Apologetics and Pastoral Theology. Principal Macleod is buried in the Grange Cemetery, Edinburgh – the Valhalla of the Free Church, as he used to describe it – directly opposite Professor John Duncan, the saintly 'Rabbi', whom he describes in *Scottish Theology* as '*one of the most profound and versatile scholars, one of the humblest of believers, and one of the most erratic and absent-minded of men!*' – a tribute which, apart from the last clause, is strikingly applicable to himself.

'*Moses my servant is dead,*' said the Lord to Joshua, '*now therefore arise.*' (Joshua 1:2).

4. No history of the building would be complete without mention of William Salvage who, for 42 years, was Janitor and Caretaker of the College and Offices.

A native of Drumbeg in Sutherland, he commenced work with the Free Church some years after the end of the first World War. Mr Salvage was always cheerful and obliging, willing to go the 'second mile', and to lend a helping hand with tasks which lay outside the duties strictly pertaining to his office. It would probably be true to say that there was nothing in his range of duties which Mr Salvage enjoyed more than his contact with the College students. Genuinely interested in their welfare, he was always ready to admit that he missed them when the College was in recess. Young and irrepressible in spirit to the very end, he was not above enlivening a dull hour with a playful prank or a practical joke, which his victims enjoyed as much as he did.

Those who knew him best had no doubt as to the genuineness of his religious

TOP
Paraphrase of the New Testament by Erasmus of Rotterdam, Oxford, 1522.

BOTTOM
The wheat and the chaff gathered into bundles. A statistical contribution towards the history of the Scottish Ecclesiastical Establishment. James McCosh, Perth, 1843.

convictions. His apprehension of spiritual truth was clear, and his delight in the Courts of Zion was evident by his regular attendance at the Sabbath and weekday services of the church. Even after illness had enfeebled him, he made valiant efforts to maintain his attendance, and his enjoyment of the Gospel message was evident.

The present writer remembers meeting William Salvage some forty years ago while attending worship in the Free Church of Scotland for the first time. He was so struck by his warm-heartedness that he can still picture in his mind's eye, even after all these years, the great welcome he received.

> *Thy saints take pleasure in her stones,*
> *Her very dust to them is dear.* (Psalm 102 (2):14).

ABOVE

De Causa Dei Contra Anti-Sabbatarios by John Brown of Wamphray, Rotterdam, 1676.

RIGHT

View from the Scott Monument showing facade of the Free Church of Scotland College and Office building, with the spire of the old Church of Scotland Assembly Hall, and the Pentland Hills in the distance.